The Jewish Experience

Liz Aylett

Hodder & Stoughton
A MEMBER OF THE HODDER HEADLINE GROUP

Acknowledgements

The Publishers would like to thank the following for permission to reproduce material in this volume:

BBC for the quote by Nathan Sharansky from *When I Get To Heaven*, 1987 and the quote by Julia Neuberger from *Open Space;* BBC/The Chief Rabbi for the extract from the broadcast by the Chief Rabbi, Radio 3, Eve of Rosh Hashanah, September 1987; Channel 4 for the quotes from *Beyond Belief*, 1987 and the quote by Gerson Cohen from *Heritage Conversation*, January 1988; Collins for the extracts from *This is My God* by Herman Wouk; Jewish Chronicle for the 2 quotations by Ida Nudel from the *Jewish Chronicle*, 1987; Vallentine Mitchell and Co Ltd for the extract from *The Diary of Anne Frank* (1954).

Every effort has been made to trace and acknowledge ownership of copyright. The publishers will be glad to make suitable arrangements with any copyright holders whom it has not been possible to contact.

British Library Cataloguing in Publication Data
Aylett, Elizabeth
    The Jewish experience
    1. Judaism
    I. Title II. Series
    296

ISBN 0 340 49371 2

First published 1991
Impression number 12 11 10 9 8 7 6 5 4
Year   1999 1998 1997 1996 1995 1994

Copyright © 1991 Liz Aylett

Typeset by Taurus Graphics, Abingdon, Oxon
Printed in Hong Kong for Hodder & Stoughton Educational, a division of Hodder Headline Plc, 338 Euston Road, London NW1 3BH by Colorcraft Ltd., Hong Kong.

The Publishers would like to thank the following for their permission to reproduce copyright photographs in this book:

The Ancient Art and Architecture Collection – pp4, 6; Associated Press – p24; Sacred Trinity Centre – p18; Barnaby's – p42l.; Werner Braun – p38; El Al – p27l.; Greg Evans – p40; Genut Audio Visual Productions – pp8, 9, 16, 19, 20, 22, 27r., 28, 32l., 32r., 4l; Judy Goldhill – p42r.; Sidney Harris/JWB – p33; Network Photographers – pp10, 35r.; Picturepoint-London – pp11, 13, 30l., 35l., 36; Popperfoto – p37; Scoop '80 – p43; Juliette Soester – pp12, 15l., 17, 21, 25, 34; Zefa – pp15r., 29, 30r.

Cover photograph supplied by Israel Government Tourist Office.

Author's note

I should like to thank the following for their kind help during the writing of this book: Esme Daniels and Rona Hart, Board of Deputies of British Jews; Rabbi Douglas Charing, Director, Jewish Education Bureau; Rev Reuben Turner, Director, JNF Publishing Co; John Wilson, Director, Sacred Trinity Centre; Susan Coller, JWB; and the Jewish people who generously shared their Faith and experiences with me, with special thanks to Karen and the two rabbis.

Contents

How Judaism Began

Do you know how many relations you have? Perhaps you belong to a small family. Or you may have many brothers, sisters, cousins, aunts, uncles. The list could go on and on. But none of your relations would have been born if it had not been for your great-grandparents. And many more – going back hundreds of years.

The Jewish people believe that they can trace their beginnings back to one person – a man called Abram. They call him the Father of the Jews. He lived nearly four thousand years ago, in the country now called Iraq.

Most people at that time **worshipped** many gods, but Abram came to believe there was just one true God. He taught his family that this God cared for them. So they should worship only Him.

When Abram was seventy-five, God told him to leave his home and travel to a new country. God promised that He would give Abram this land and that his **descendants** would become a great nation. In return, Abram and all his family were to obey and worship Him.

Abram was puzzled. He had no children. How could he have any descendants now? However, he trusted God. So he and his wife, Sarah, set off towards Canaan. His nephew's family went too.

The whole family settled in Canaan and were known as Hebrews. This comes from a word meaning 'from the other side', because they came from the other side of the River Euphrates. They did not forget their promise to worship God.

And then Sarah had a son. They were amazed; Sarah was ninety years old at the time! They called the boy Isaac, which means 'laughter'. Abram was given a new name, Abraham, 'father of the people'.

God tested Abraham by ordering him to **sacrifice** Isaac. You can see Abraham with his knife raised, ready to strike. But God sent an angel to stop him. Abraham sacrificed a ram instead.

Many years after Abraham's death, there was **famine** in Canaan. The Hebrews moved to Egypt, where there was plenty of food. At first, everything went well. But later the Egyptians used them as slaves to build two great new cities.

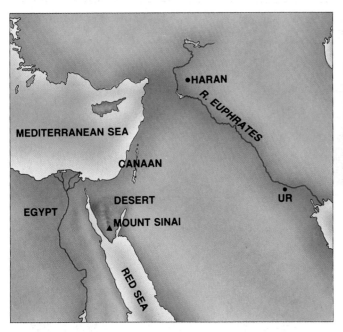

Map of the Middle East in Abraham's time. Abraham was born in Ur and moved to Haran when he was young.

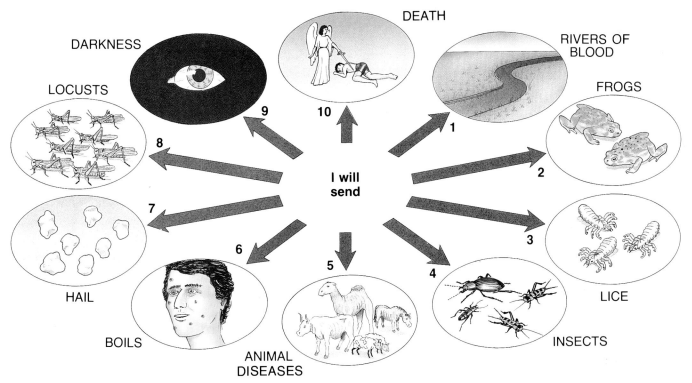

The ten plagues. See how each one is more horrible than the one before.

Later, the Hebrews became known as the Israelites. Their great leader was Moses. He asked the Pharaoh of Egypt to set the slaves free. The Pharaoh refused; slaves were useful. At last, however, God sent ten horrible plagues and the Pharaoh finally let the Israelites go.

They escaped into the desert, an event known as the Exodus. There, they lived for forty years, while trying to return to Canaan. Moses died during this time. So a man called Joshua led them back into the land God had promised to them.

The people were divided into twelve tribes and the land was shared between them. Each tribe was named after one of Abraham's great-grandsons. One of the tribes was called Judah.

1 a) Copy the map of the Middle East in Abraham's time.
  b) Mark in the journeys in this chapter.
2 a) Write down the meaning of the names Abraham and Isaac.
  b) Why do you think Isaac was given his name?
  c) Where do you think the name Judaism comes from?
  d) Read Genesis 32:24–29 and 35:10. Who do you think the stranger was?
  e) Why do you think Jacob's name was changed?

3 Which of the following words do you think describe Abraham? Give a reason for each choice.
  brave; foolish; old; obedient; cruel; friendly; trusting; bloodthirsty.
4 Abraham was willing to give up his son because God told him to. Write a paragraph about something important to you which you would only give up if you really felt you had to.
5 Divide into groups, with one person taking the part of Abraham. Show how you think Abraham would have tried to persuade the others to leave their homes and come with you to an unknown land.

2 Jewish Holy Books

Moses is important to Christians as well as to Jews. This sculpture of him is by the Roman Catholic artist Michelangelo.

In Exodus chapter 19 we read that God called Moses to the top of a mountain. God told Moses that He had chosen the Israelites as His special people. He repeated the promise made to Abraham, that He would look after them and lead them to a new land.

In return they had to keep God's commandments and to set a good example to all people. Moses was given two stone tablets with the most important rules written on them. These are the Ten Commandments.

Every summer the Jews celebrate this event at the festival of Shavuot. The **synagogues** are decorated with flowers. The Jews thank God for these and for the Torah. Here is a special poem for Shavuot.

▶ Could we with ink the ocean fill,
  Were every blade of grass a **quill,**
  Were the world of **parchment** made,
  And every man a **scribe** by trade,
  To write the love of God above
  Would drain the ocean dry,
  Nor would the scroll contain the whole
  Though stretched from sky to sky.

You can read the story of Abraham in the Book of Genesis. This is the first book in the Jewish Bible. But the Bible is not just a collection of stories. For the Jewish people, it is much more important than that.

You may belong to a club or society. There is probably a set of rules for all the members. The rules will have been drawn up by members of the club, maybe many years ago. Often, the rules are written down in a book.

The Jews have special books, in which they can read all the rules of their religion. The oldest of these is the Bible, the Tenach. This is really a collection of twenty-four books. Christians call them the Old Testament.

For Jews, the most important part of the Tenach is the first five books. These are called the Torah. It means teaching. The Torah is a mixture of stories and **commandments**. It describes the **creation** of the world and the early history of the Jews, ending with the death of Moses.

The Classroom Commandment.

There are 613 commandments in the Torah! Many of them deal with the Temple sacrifices. Today there is no Temple; there are no sacrifices. So those laws no longer apply. But the others teach Jews what they should do in just about every part of their lives. For this Jewish lady, the Torah is much more than a book:

▶ The commandments in the Torah are my guide to living. The stories in the Torah really happened, the people in the Torah are real people that I can identify with.

I firmly believe in the Torah as a complete way of life. I don't consider it to be a holy way of life. It is simply my way of life.

Another holy book is called the Talmud. It means study. It gives advice from early Jewish leaders who studied the Torah. They worked out rules to help Jews to keep the commandments.

1 Match the words on the left to their meaning:

The Torah	study of the Torah
The Tenach	teaching
The Talmud	book which tells the story of Moses
Exodus	the Jewish Bible

2 Find the Ten Commandments in Exodus 20.
   a) Make 3 columns on a page.
      (i) In the left-hand one write the numbers 1–10, one for each Commandment.
      (ii) Look at the drawings on the left and decide which drawing fits which Commandment. Put the letter of the drawing in the second column, next to the correct number.
      (iii) In the third column write *yes* if the person in the drawing is obeying the Commandment, and *no* if they are not.
   b) The last five Commandments begin with 'do not'. Rewrite each one so that it starts with 'Always'. For example, number eight might become:
      Always leave other people's belongings alone.
   c) Pick any one Commandment. Give reasons why you think it is important today.
3 Look at the picture of the classroom. What do you think is the difference between the commandment and the rules?
4 a) In groups, make up two commandments for your class. Give reasons for each.
   b) Work out two or three rules which will show people how to keep each of your commandments.

3 What Jews Believe

The Jewish belief about God can be put very simply. There is only one God. He created the world and He sees and knows everything.

God gave them His laws for two reasons. First, so that they would know how to worship Him. Second, so that they would be able to show other people how to live in a kind and caring way. Jews believe that this relationship with God will continue only so long as they remain faithful to Judaism.

The idea that there is only one God has a special name. It is called monotheism. The first Hebrew which a Jewish child learns is a prayer called the Shema. This is part of the Torah, and the first words sum up the belief in one God.

▶ Hear, O Israel, the Lord our God, the Lord is One, and you shall love the Lord your God with all your heart and with all your soul and with all your might.

Deuteronomy 6:4–5

Do not hold back the wages of someone you have hired, not even for one night

Do not cheat when you use weights and measures

If a fellow Israelite's donkey or cow has fallen down, don't ignore it, help him to get the animal to its feet again

The Torah gives examples of how to treat other people.

The Shema should also be the last thing a Jew says before death. Herman Wouk's experience shows that this is not as unlikely as it may sound.

▶ I used to wonder whether a man could really call to mind and recite the Creed (Shema). Then once, during a **typhoon** in the Pacific, I was almost blown off the deck of a ship. I remember quite clearly thinking, as I went sliding towards my fate, 'Well, if I drown, let me say the Shema as I go'.

Herman Wouk: *This is my God*

God watches over the world and cares for all the people in it. Jews try to follow God's example. One way to do this is to treat other people as we should like them to treat us. The Torah says:

▶ Do not take revenge on anyone or continue to hate him, but love your neighbour as you love yourself.

This child takes time to visit an elderly man.

Sadly, people do not always think about others. But the Jews look forward to the coming of the Messiah, God's messenger of peace. Then everyone will obey God's commandments. When this happens, the whole world will be at peace.

Christians believe that Jesus was the Messiah. But the Jews look at the world today and say that they are still waiting. They are waiting for a human being who will be so special that he will bring everyone together.

God has told Jews how to get the most out of their lives. But the end of life on earth does not mean the end of everything. There will be another kind of life which lasts forever, although nobody knows what it will be like.

Belief in an afterlife is an excellent reason for leading a good life on earth. This belief is strong in most religions. A Jewish girl wrote:

▶ I believe that there is a Heaven. I think that once we die, we do go to Heaven. After reading the Torah it is obvious that G_d loves us too much to end our lives after we die.

You will notice that she does not write out all the letters of God's name. Jews believe that His name is holy. This means they must treat it with respect. Some Jews prefer not to write out the whole name. They feel it would insult God if the paper with His name on were torn or dropped.

In this book, we will write God in full. But remember that any Jewish pupils among you would like God's name to be treated carefully.

This is Shabbetai Zevi being led into a city. He claimed to be the Messiah. The people welcomed him. Later they realised his claim was false.

1 Copy out these sentences, using the correct word or words from the brackets:
a) The Jews believe in (one God/many gods).
b) The Jewish people were (punished/chosen) to set a good example to others.
c) The first prayer a Jewish child learns is the (Torah/Shema).
2 Why does the Jewish girl believe there must be a Heaven?
3 What will the world be like when the Messiah comes?

4 a) Write a paragraph about someone you know of who tries to treat others as they would like to be treated.
b) Write a few lines about a time when you have not done this.
c) What do you think you should have done?
d) Write down your own example of how to treat other people.
e) Draw a picture of somebody following your example.

4 Orthodox and Reform Jews

These are Hasidic Jews. They keep the Law very strictly. Notice their traditional fur hats and long coats.

For thousands of years Jews lived in the way the Torah told them to. About two hundred years ago, a few Jews felt that some laws were out of date. They thought Judaism should be modernised. They were called Reform Jews.

Reform Jews believe that God gave the Torah. But that was thousands of years ago. People do not live in the same way now. So Reform Jews keep studying the Torah and sometimes change laws, or even drop them altogether.

Other Jews believe that they should not make any changes to the laws. These are Orthodox Jews. This is how one of them feels about the Torah.

▶ We believe that you can't **negate** any of the laws. The fact that these laws have been the same for three thousand years is the only reason why there is still a Jewish religion today Once you start changing them you're changing the whole religion and it ceases to exist.

Orthodox Jews believe that the laws show them how to cope with everything. If there is a problem, the leading Jews must study the Holy Books to find an answer.

Take Lord Jakobovits, for example. He once worked as a rabbi in New York. To reach the synagogue, you could use the stairs or the lift. But, on the Sabbath, Jews must not work machinery. And it was difficult for elderly and disabled people to climb all the stairs.

The rabbi installed a time-switch. Now his **congregation** could use the lift on the Sabbath without breaking the commandment. A Jewish newspaper made fun of him for doing this. He replied:

▶ You never tire of complaining that Orthodox leaders are out of tune with the times. Yet when the occasion presents itself for you to acknowledge an effort to [make Jewish laws easier to observe] by the use of the most up-to-date scientific advances, you do not like it either.

Immanuel Jakobovits: *Journal of a Rabbi*

How Orthodox and Reform Jews feel about the Torah.

There are now non-Orthodox Jews in many countries. They are called Reform, Liberal, Progressive or Conservative. They are not exactly the same as each other, but in this book they are all called Reform. A rabbi sums up what it means to be a member of a Reform community.

▶ We believe that there has to be a balance between living in a modern world, with all the challenges that it brings, and living with the traditions and the values of Judaism. Sometimes we have to pull the two together and see what is the best sense we can make out of it.

A choir in a Reform synagogue. Notice that there are men and women. There may be an organ as well.

One big difference between Reform and Orthodox Judaism is that men and women are treated differently. Three Jews explain some of the ways. The first two are Orthodox.

▶ (In the synagogue), the ladies are upstairs, the men are down here. The reason is that in Temple times it was already felt that it was not right for men and women to be praying together. It was feared that the men's attention might wander from the adoration of the Divine to the adoration of the women.

▶ We do have very different laws (for men and women) within the Orthodox religion. But it doesn't mean that we're not equal, just different. The men have more laws regarding the **community**, the women have more laws regarding the home.

▶ I found difficulties as a woman watching from the balcony at what was going on, and not feeling very involved. I find that in a Reform synagogue men and women do exactly the same, both in the actual synagogue service and in the governing of the community.

In this book you will find many ways in which Orthodox and Reform Jews are different. But remember that it is what Jews have in common which is most important. They share the belief in one God. They try to set a good example to others.

1 a) Why was Reform Judaism started?
   b) What do Reform and Orthodox Jews have in common?
2 a) In you own words, give an Orthodox reason for not changing the laws.
   b) Do you agree with it? Give reasons.
3 a) Why do you think the laws about women are mainly to do with the home?
   b) Do you think men and women should play equal parts in the synagogue and the community? Give reasons for and against.
4 a) Write down three ways in which girls and boys are expected to do different things at your school or in your home.
   b) What do you think is the reason for each difference?
   c) Do you agree with each reason? Say why.
5 a) Write a paragraph about three modern problems where it is difficult to decide what is right and what is wrong. Show that you understand why it is so difficult. (Some ideas to help you: nuclear weapons, unborn babies, pollution.)
   b) How would (i) Orthodox and (ii) Reform Jews go about finding an answer to each problem?

5 *The Life Cycle:* From birth to Bar Mitzvah

A baby is born! For most families, this is a marvellous reason for a celebration. In Jewish families, a special ceremony takes place. The child is given at least one Hebrew and one ordinary name. There are special prayers, too. Boy babies are **circumcised**, because God told Abraham:

▶ And he that is eight days old shall be circumcised among you, every male throughout the generations.
Genesis 17:10–12

Karen, an Orthodox **Jewess**, explains her feelings when her babies were named.

▶ I felt part of an enormous family when my chidren were given their Hebrew names, and that I was carrying on a wonderful tradition. Our children were named in memory of our **deceased** relatives, so that they live on in our children.

Children can go to special classes where they will learn about their religion. They often take place on a Sunday. Even three-year-olds can go. The Talmud includes advice to teachers.

Children in a Jewish nursery school. Notice the Hebrew letters.

▶ Do not threaten a child; either punish him or forgive him.
A classroom should never have more than 25 pupils. There are four categories of pupil: the sponge – he absorbs and retains everything; the funnel – everything that goes in comes out; the sifter – he remembers the trivial and forgets the significant; the sieve – he retains the important and sifts out the incidental.

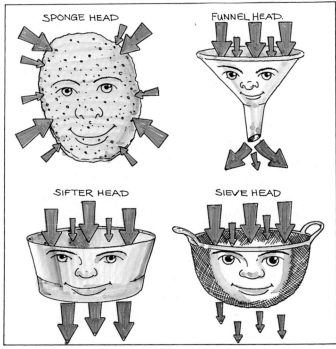

Which kind of pupil are you?

Children are told about Abraham and Moses, as well as other people who have been important in the history of Judaism. They also learn to understand why Jews live and worship in the ways they do. Some lessons are spent learning to read and speak Hebrew.

This may be hard for some children, just as learning a foreign language may be difficult for them at secondary school. But, for most of them, it is worth it! One Jewish girl explains what it meant to her.

▶ I must have been about six or seven when I could read a little bit of Hebrew. I felt thrilled. I think being Jewish it is important to read Hebrew because God's book, the Torah, is written in Hebrew.

This boy is reading from the Torah at a practice for his Bar Mitzvah ceremony. See the pointer he uses, so he does not mark the precious scroll.

Jewish boys and girls have a special birthday soon after they start secondary school. It is thirteen for a boy and twelve for a girl. A boy becomes Bar Mitzvah; a girl becomes Bat Mitzvah. It means Son (or Daughter) of the Commandments.

From now on it is their **responsibility** to carry out their duties to their family and their religion. Nobody is going to remind them!

It's a very special event. So most families hold a celebration. Relatives often come a long way; maybe from Israel or America. The whole family may attend a ceremony at the synagogue.

Boys read from the Torah for the first time. They spend a lot of time practising the part that they will read. Reform synagogues also allow girls to do this. In most Orthodox communities it is still forbidden.

An Orthodox girl describes her special day.

▶ I became Bat Mitzvah on the twentieth of June. I felt extremely nervous but yet excited. I had been looking forward to this day for many years. Today I would become a Daughter of the Law. This meant a lot to me.

When I actually got on to the **bimah**, my nervousness seemed to die down and my adrenalin seemed to take over. It increased my excitement and I enjoyed it very much. After my Bat Mitzvah I felt like an adult member of our community.

1 a) Draw this grid in your book and fill in the answers, using the clues below.

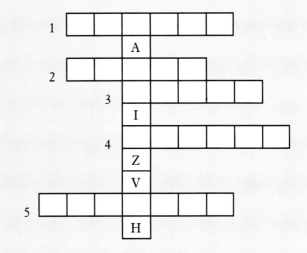

(i) The language of the Torah.
(ii) First five books of the Tenach.
(iii) He led the Exodus.
(iv) The study of the Torah.
(v) Father of the Jews.
b) Now, write the word which goes down. Why is this important to young Jews?

2 a) Why did Karen name her children after dead relatives?
b) Do you think this is a good idea? Give reasons.

3 a) What do Jewish children learn at religion school?
b) Why do they (i) learn Jewish history and (ii) learn to read Hebrew?

4 Read what the Talmud says about schools and schoolchildren.
a) Are the two rules kept in your school?
b) Do you think they are good rules? Give your reasons.
c) Which kind of pupil would you like to be? Give reasons.

5 a) Write a paragraph describing how you think a Jewish boy feels when he becomes Bar Mitzvah.
b) Write a paragraph about a day in your life which was special. Explain why it was important and how you felt.

6 The Sabbath

NO WORK ON THE SABBATH

REFORM JEWS ARE NOT SO STRICT EG. THEY MAY DRIVE TO THE SYNAGOGUE

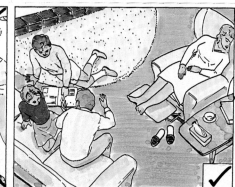

Every week, Jews celebrate something which happened a very long time ago – the beginning of the whole **universe**. Jews believe that God created the world in six days. He rested on the seventh day. It's called the Sabbath.

The fourth Commandment says, 'Remember the Sabbath Day, to keep it holy. In it thou shalt not do any work'. So the Sabbath is a special day for Jews.

It is a whole day which is different from the others. A day for a special meal, a family get-together, best clothes, a complete break from normal routine.

The Jewish Sabbath begins at sunset on a Friday evening and ends at nightfall on Saturday. In the Jewish calendar, a new day starts at sunset because the Torah says, 'The evening and the morning created He them'. For Orthodox Jews, the time varies with the seasons of the year, but many Reform Jews have a fixed starting time.

Herman Wouk, an American playwright,

describes his feelings. He has left the theatre in the middle of a rehearsal to get home for the beginning of the Sabbath.

▶ Leaving the gloomy theatre, the shouting stage-hands and the dense tobacco smoke, I have come home. It has been a startling change, very like a return from the wars.

My wife and my boys are waiting for me dressed in best clothes. We have sat down to a splendid dinner. My wife and I have caught up with our week's conversation. The boys, knowing that the Sabbath is the occasion for asking questions, have asked them. The Bible, the encyclopedia, the atlas, have piled up on the table.

Herman Wouk: *This is my God*

The word Sabbath means rest, but in many Jewish homes, and certainly in Orthodox ones, a great deal of hard work is done before the day begins.

The house must be clean and tidy, the Sabbath meal ready, the table laid with flowers and best plates and glasses, and the wine uncorked. Even the candlesticks have been specially polished. Everyone tries to do something to help.

And nobody forgets that this is a holy day. The Sabbath candles are lit as the Sabbath begins. Usually the mother does this. She recites a blessing as she does so. But in Sandy's home:

▶ The girls light their own candle, as their contribution towards **Shabbat**. It makes them an important part of the home. It's not just watching somebody else do something. They are involved.

Candlelight is different from electric light. It **signifies** peace coming into the house.

The Sabbath meal. Notice the wine and candles.

When the father and Bar Mitzvah boys come home from synagogue, the whole family wish each other a happy Sabbath. The father blesses God, the Creator of the Sabbath. The blessing is usually made over wine, because it is a special occasion. This event is called Kiddush.

The father blesses the Sabbath, his children and two specially baked loaves called Hallot. He also recites some verses from the Tenach. This is one way for a Jewish husband to thank his wife for everything she does. After the meal, everyone thanks God for what they have enjoyed. An Orthodox Jewish girl explains why the Sabbath is important in her family.

▶ Our family looks forward to Shabbat because it is a time when we are all together. Our family get together on the Friday night and have a large meal.

We all enjoy this very much because we can talk about what has happened to us during the week; and we talk about the future and the past. The Sabbath is when the fast pace of the week slows down and we all relax and enjoy ourselves.

1 Complete each of these sentences using the correct ending from the list on the right.

a) Sabbath begins   in advance.
b) Blessing God over wine   is on Friday.
c) The main Sabbath meal   is called Kiddush.
d) The meal must be cooked   at sunset on Friday.

2 a) Make a list of jobs which need to be done before the Sabbath begins.
b) Put a tick beside the ones which could be done by someone of your age.

3 a) Read what Herman Wouk and the girl say about the Sabbath.
b) Write down the words from this list which you think describe the Sabbath. For each one, explain your choice.
happy; solemn; calm; relaxed; frantic; enjoyable; special; noisy; thoughtful.

4 a) Read Proverbs 31. Pick out 3 lines from the passage and put them in more up-to-date language so they would describe a wife of today.
b) What do you do to show your mother that you appreciate her?

The end of the Sabbath. Look for the spice box – Jews hope its sweetness will last for the whole week.

7 Jewish Family Life

▶ If we as Jews have survived as a people it is not because we have had mighty armies or great statesmen. It is because we've had **stable** homes and we grew up in places in which the feeling of happiness made up for many of the problems outside.

Lord Jakobovits

If your next-door neighbour has a poster in his window saying VOTE FOR SMITH on a red background you know he supports the Labour Party. A football fan with a red and white scarf may be off to cheer Liverpool. And a house with one of these

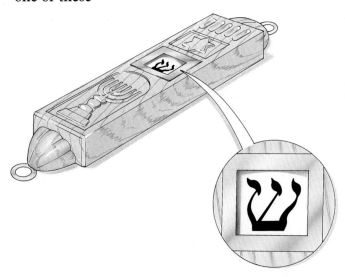

nailed to the right-hand doorpost belongs to a Jewish family.

The Shema tells Jews that they should 'write them (words from the Shema) upon the doorposts of your houses and upon your gates'. In the early days, Jews engraved the words on the doorpost. Later, they found it was more practical to write on a scroll. They made a hole in the doorpost and put the scroll inside. For many hundreds of years, however, Jews have used a special case, like the one in the picture above.

It contains a tiny parchment scroll, called a mezuzah, with the first part of the Shema written on it. The mezuzah shows visitors that it is a Jewish home. But its main purpose is to remind the family that God is always with them. So they should obey his commandments at all times.

Through the small window, you can see a Hebrew letter, the first letter in the Hebrew word for Almighty, one of the names given to God. Some Jews touch the mezuzah case when they enter or leave. This is a sign of respect for God's word.

The case in the left-hand picture has a candlestick called a menorah. It reminds Jews of the one which used to be in the Temple in Jerusalem. Some mezuzah cases are made of gold or ivory. But a plain wooden or plastic one is just as good.

Moving day! A rabbi fixes a mezuzah to the doorpost. Below it is the Blessing for the house.

Home is a special place. Perhaps you have looked forward to getting home to tell your family that your team has won a match, so they would know how pleased you feel. Or maybe you've had a row with your friends and wanted to tell someone at home all about it.

Home is where we learned to talk, walk, feed ourselves, and play with toys. Those with brothers and sisters probably learned how to fight and then make friends again. Our parents or guardians take care of us and teach us the things they feel we need to know.

In a Jewish home. The picture by the window shows the direction of Jerusalem. Jews face this way when they pray.

It's the same in anybody's home. But what makes Jewish homes special is that Jewish parents want their children to follow the ways of Judaism. So the home is the place to learn what it means to be Jewish.

The Jewish father must:
- support his family
- study the Torah
- see that his children study the Torah.

The mother must:
- feed the family as the Torah instructs
- make sure her husband and sons have the right clothes
- prepare the home for the Sabbath and the festivals
- teach her daughters what they will need to know when they have their own homes.

Of course, in many families, especially in Reform homes, these jobs may be shared differently. But Orthodox mothers take their responsibilities very seriously. Karen and Sandy explain:

▶ Having children has made me more aware of my Judaism, because I have to make sure my children are aware of their **obligations**. I have to make sure my household is arranged to back up the instructions they receive in their religion school.

▶ The central point of the Jewish religion is the home. The home is where the children are brought up, where the education takes place. Where the **rituals** of Shabbat and the festivals take place.

And therefore, as the woman is called 'the **foundation** of the home', really I would say that the woman is the most important thing in Judaism.

1 a) What is a mezuzah?
   b) What does it remind Jews about?
   c) Design your own mezuzah case. You don't have to have a menorah – your own patterns will do.
2 Which of these words describe a Jewish mother's feelings about her place in the home? For each, explain your choice. proud; not bothered; caring; worried; responsible; ashamed; important.
3 a) Write a paragraph on the part played by the mother in many Jewish homes.
   b) Why do you think Sandy calls the woman 'the most important thing in Judaism?
   c) What do you think are the most important things *your* mother does?
   d) Do you think a man could do all these tasks just as well as a woman? Give your reasons for each.

Food

Everybody needs food and drink. Most people have some idea which things are good for them and which are not. We are guided by what doctors and other experts say, and, of course, by what we like or dislike. But there are so many things to choose from, it isn't always easy to decide.

Jews don't have quite such a problem. The Torah states clearly what they must not eat. It tells them how to kill the permitted animals as painlessly as possible. And it tells them they must soak meat before they cook it so that all the blood is removed.

It may seem strange that a religion tells its followers what they can eat, but Jewish people do not think so. Remember that they have promised to obey God's word in everything. Keeping the laws about food is one way of showing that they are doing this.

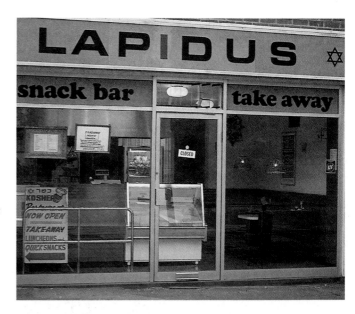

Eating kosher food is no problem if you live near this take-away in Manchester.

Reform Jews believe that some of the food laws are no longer necessary. But Orthodox Jews feel they are just as important today as when they were first given.

An important rule is that dishes with meat cannot be eaten at the same meal as ones with milk in them. Orthodox Jewish kitchens have separate pots and pans for cooking milk and meat recipes.

Children do not always understand the reasons for things they can and cannot do. One little boy asked what would happen if he ate a Kit-Kat straight after his chicken. After all, he had seen his friends eating chocolate after meat and nothing happened to them.

His mother explained that nothing terrible would happen to him. It was just that, because they are Jewish, there are some things they do differently from other people.

Food which has been prepared according to the laws is called kosher food. It means 'fit' to eat. It is not always easy to buy kosher food, especially in country areas.

But Jewish families know that, by following the laws about food, they are helping to keep the special promise made to God. Every meal, especially on the Sabbath, reminds them of that promise.

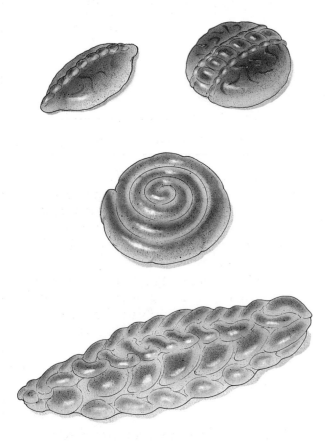

Plaited loaves for the Sabbath and festivals.

Clothes

Most Jewish teenagers wear whatever they want to, or whatever their parents will buy for them! But for weekday morning prayers, Jewish men, and boys over thirteen, carry out some special instructions from the Torah.

The boy may have woken up thinking about the James Bond film he saw the night before, or the homework he forgot to do. But, while putting on his kippa, tallit and tefillin, he will have plenty of time to think about what they mean. So he is now ready to concentrate on his prayers.

Kippa – skull cap.
My children wear their kippa whenever we're doing anything holy. Whenever we're having any of our ceremonies at home; whenever we're in synagogue; whenever it's a holy day; whenever they open a holy book.

Tefillin – boxes containing words from the Shema.
Tie them on your arms and wear them on your foreheads as a reminder.

The Shema

Tallit – prayer shawl.
Tell them to make fringes in the borders of their garments, so they may look upon them and remember all the commandments of the Lord.

Numbers 15:38–39

1 a) Copy out this paragraph and fill in the missing words.
Jewish men may cover their _____ at certain times. Some wear a skullcap called a _____ all the time. Their tallit has _____ to remind them of God's _____ .
At some prayer times they also wear tefillin, one near the _____ , the other near the heart.
b) Do you have clothes or other objects which you have to wear at certain times? Describe them and explain when and why you wear them.
c) Do you think it is a good idea to have to put on these special things? Give your reasons.

2 Read Deuteronomy 14:3–21.
a) Make two columns on a page. Head one column *yes* for permitted foods and the other *no* for foods which are not allowed. Then put these foods in the correct column:
lamb chops; prawn-flavoured crisps; pork sausages; chicken curry and rice; cod and chips; ham and mushroom pizza; roast beef and Yorkshire pudding; ravioli on toast.
b) In groups, plan a three-course meal for an Orthodox Jewish family. You may have as many vegetables and fruit as you wish.
c) Compare your menus with the rest of your class and pick the best one.

8 At the Synagogue

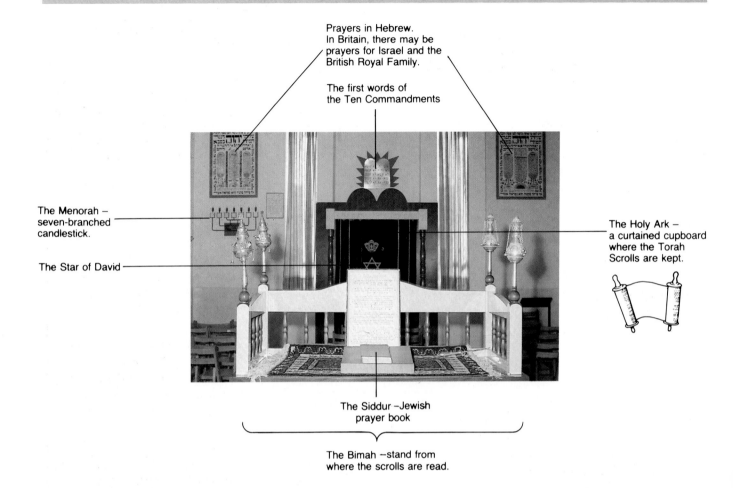

Prayers in Hebrew.
In Britain, there may be prayers for Israel and the British Royal Family.

The first words of the Ten Commandments

The Menorah – seven-branched candlestick.

The Star of David

The Holy Ark – a curtained cupboard where the Torah Scrolls are kept.

The Siddur –Jewish prayer book

The Bimah –stand from where the scrolls are read.

The synagogue is the meeting place for Jews. It is where they pray, study, and talk. The building may be large or small, old or modern. It may be anywhere in the world. But certain things will be the same. You can see them in the picture above.

Jews do their best to go to the Sabbath services. Orthodox men attend on Friday evening and then return home for the meal. Reform synagogues usually have later services so the whole family can go after they have eaten. Saturday morning services are for everybody.

Any member of the congregation can lead them through the order of service found in the siddur, the Jewish prayer-book. It does not have to be a rabbi. But in an Orthodox synagogue it is always a man. In a Reform synagogue, a woman or man may be the leader.

A synagogue in England.

Most synagogues, however, do have a rabbi. This is always a man in Orthodox synagogues but there are several women Reform rabbis. An Orthodox rabbi describes what happens in his synagogue.

▶ We have readings from the Psalms. We have special prayers and a reading from the Torah. During the morning service we go up, take out one of the scrolls, and take it up to the reader's desk. Then I will open up the scroll and read from it in Hebrew.

At the end I hold up the scroll, and say a prayer in English for Her Majesty followed by a prayer for the State of Israel. Then we take the scroll down again and put it back into the Ark. The Ark is closed. After the service, we usually have a gathering of the congregation in the hall. We have Kiddush over wine and cakes.

In an Orthodox synagogue, nearly all the service is in Hebrew. Only the prayer for the Royal Family and the **sermon** are in English. In Reform synagogues there is more English, as a Reform rabbi explains.

▶ There is some English in our service. The main parts of the service, such as the Shema, would nearly always be in Hebrew. In my service, I try to have something like seventy-five per cent Hebrew, twenty-five per cent English.

Jewish men should also pray every evening, morning and afternoon. The prayers can be held in the synagogue as long as there are at least ten males over the age of thirteen present.

Most people lead such busy lives that it is impossible to get to their synagogue as often as this. But they can pray anywhere. The important thing is that they really mean what they say.

Prayer is a way of talking to God. Sometimes people who are not religious think that praying just means asking God for something which they want, like a BMX bike or good exam results. But those are selfish prayers. When Jewish people pray, they:

- praise God for His creation
- ask Him to care for people in trouble
- thank Him for looking after everyone
- ask Him to forgive them for doing wrong
- pray for peace all over the world

These children have been visiting a synagogue in Manchester. There were over 30 000 Jews in Greater Manchester in 1985.

WESTON ORTHODOX SYNAGOGUE

SABBATH SERVICES THIS WEEK:

FRIDAY   4.10 p.m.
SATURDAY   9–11.45 a.m.

LADIES & CHILDREN →
← MEN

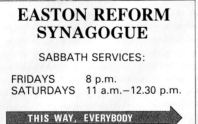

EASTON REFORM SYNAGOGUE

SABBATH SERVICES:

FRIDAYS   8 p.m.
SATURDAYS   11 a.m.–12.30 p.m.

THIS WAY, EVERYBODY →

Differences between the Orthodox and the Reform synagogues.

1 a) Draw each of the following objects in a synagogue. (i) the menorah; (ii) the Torah scrolls; (iii) the Commandments.
   b) For each one, explain why it is important.
2 Divide your page into two columns. Head one column *Orthodox* and the other *Reform*. Copy these statements into the correct column. (Careful: some statements may belong to both.) Pages 10–11 may help.
   a) I worship one God.
   b) My synagogue allows women rabbis.
   c) I don't sit with my husband in the synagogue.
   d) Our Sabbath Eve service starts at different times each week.
   e) Our whole family goes to the synagogue after the Sabbath meal.
3 a) Write down five things Jews think about when they pray.
   b) Now make up your own prayer, with one sentence for each of the five things. You might begin: I praise you God for. . . . Make sure you use your own words, and talk about things in your own life.
4 Find out where your nearest synagogue is. In groups, write a letter to the rabbi, asking if you may visit his synagogue. Then, as a class, pick the best letter and send it.

9 Rabbis

A minister in a synagogue is called a rabbi. It means 'my teacher'. The greater part of the rabbi's job is to teach his congregation to understand the Jewish way of life.

A Reform rabbi describes his work

▶ The rabbi's job is very largely teaching. You spend many hours teaching, both adults and children. But it goes further than that. You teach through your example. Your sermons should be teaching sermons. Your **conduct** is also a source of teaching.

You also have a responsibility for people's **welfare**. Making hospital calls is part of your duties. People who are sick are entitled to a visit from the rabbi. People who have got some difficulty should feel that the rabbi is available and can help.

Sometimes there may be a Jewish patient in hospital. [The nurses] are very concerned that they do the right thing when it comes to his diet. If it comes to his death, they may be very frightened of breaking laws. So you have got to give them instruction.

You are an ambassador to the outside world. It is important to go to schools to speak about Judaism.

The ritual of the community is your responsibility. If the wrong thing is done in a service it's your fault. You also have a [duty] to write articles, and to make announcements.

You should make sure that people in the community feel that they are useful. For example, most of the members of my staff are **volunteers**.

[What gives me special pleasure is] a job well done. For example, in the case of a funeral. If you feel that you've helped a family, that the whole thing has been done in the best possible way, that can give you a sense of satisfaction.

An Orthodox rabbi describes his work

▶ My parish work is basically the same as any other minister. Visiting the sick, burying the dead, marrying those who wish to be married, seeing to the **spiritual** requirements that people have.

I go to the local jail and see the Jewish prisoners there. There is also a place for mentally retarded children. I go there and give them religious instruction.

If a person feels he has some problem that he wants to share, I certainly will listen to him. I can try to guide him along the right path, as far as is possible. Beyond that there is nothing that I can do that another person couldn't do equally well.

I am not God's policeman, it's not my job to chase people up. I myself try to keep everything very strictly and I like to think that my members do so too.

What makes me happy is when I see that a child who comes from a not very **observant** home is suddenly taking an interest in his religion and taking it seriously.

How a rabbi dresses for most services. For New Year services he wears white, a symbol of purity.

1 a) Which of these words describes the kind of person a rabbi should be:
a good listener; thin; bad-tempered; kind; like a policeman; hard-working; a good example; thoughtful; impatient.
Give your reasons for each choice.

2 Pick out three people or groups of people a rabbi may see in his work. For each one, write a sentence explaining how he will try to help them.

3 a) Describe the rabbi's clothes.

b) Why do you think a rabbi wears white clothes for New Year?

4 Why do you think a person may become a rabbi? Try to think of at least two reasons.

5 In groups, make up an advertisement for a rabbi of a Reform synagogue. In your own words say what kind of person you are looking for. Compare your adverts with the rest of your class and decide which is the best.

The Life Cycle: Marriage and Death

These Jews have come from Russia, where they were not allowed a Jewish wedding ceremony. They are now in America, where their marriages are blessed under twenty six huppahs, one for each couple.

A wedding is one of the happiest occasions in Jewish life. But it is also a serious one. The bride and groom are about to start a new Jewish home. Their children will begin a new generation of Jews.

Most people would not marry unless they were in love with each other. But other things matter, too. Sharing is one of the most important parts of marriage. People who have nothing or very little in common may have problems.

For example, imagine being married to someone who spoke a different language, or who wanted to spend all their spare time playing darts when you just wanted to watch television. Being in love does not always mean that life together will be plain sailing.

Orthodox Jews could not live according to the Torah if they did not marry other Jews. There would be problems for many Reform Jews too. Rosalind, an Orthodox Jewess explains:

▶ Religion as such is not so important in our marriage, but our **culture** and tradition is, regarding festivals and food, [for example].

She does not mean that religious beliefs do not matter. It's just that living with someone who had different ideas about everyday life would be difficult. So most British Jews do marry other Jews.

At an Orthodox wedding, the bride joins the groom under the huppah. This is a canopy on four poles which represents the couple's future home. It shows that the groom will look after his future bride.

The rabbi talks to the couple about their marriage. He blesses them, and they drink wine from the same goblet. This shows that they are going to share a life together. The groom places a ring on the bride's finger. He says in Hebrew 'Behold you are now married to me, with this ring, according to the Law of Moses and Israel.' She is now his wife.

The rabbi reads the Ketubah, the marriage agreement. It says that the groom has promised to take care of his wife.

The rabbi then recites seven blessings over the couple. He ends by praising God 'who has created joy and gladness, bridegroom and bride, love and brotherhood, pleasure and delight, peace and harmony.'

The final event may come as a surprise. The groom crushes a wine-glass on the floor with his heel! This is a reminder that the Temple in Jerusalem was destroyed many years ago. The newly-weds, too, will have to face bad times together as well as good.

The whole congregation shouts 'Mazel Tov!', which means 'Good Luck!'. The service is over. Everyone joins the newly-weds for a wedding party.

The last stage in the life cycle is death. Jewish burials take place as quickly as possible. Jews believe that rich and poor are equal after death, so the service is the same for everyone.

The coffin is plain and there are usually no flowers. Orthodox Jews are always buried, but some Reform synagogues allow **cremation**. In Orthodox families, close relations make a small tear in their clothes to show their unhappiness.

The family of the dead person is expected to spend the next week at home. They are encouraged to talk about how they feel. Friends bring food for them, so they do not need to cook. The men do not shave and the women do not wear make-up. They may sit on low stools and wear slippers. This shows that their normal life has been interrupted by the death.

Every year, on the anniversary of the death of a parent, the children light a candle and say a special prayer called the Kaddish. But it does not mention the dead person. Instead, it praises God and asks for peace:

▶ Blessed, praised and glorified be the Name of the Holy One, blessed be He. He who makes peace in His high places, may He make peace for us and for all Israel, and say Amen.

These are Jewish **headstones**. Notice the Hebrew writing and the Star of David.

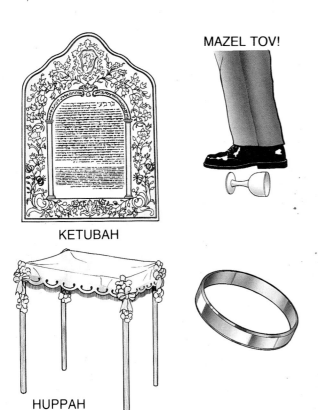

MAZEL TOV!

KETUBAH

HUPPAH

1 a) Copy the pictures on the left of objects used in an Orthodox Jewish wedding, but put them in the order they are used.
   b) Describe what each is used for.
2 a) Do you think it is easier or harder to be friends with someone who likes the same things as you do? Give your reasons.
   b) Why do Jews usually marry other Jews?
3 a) What do close relations do after someone in a Jewish family dies?
   b) Say what each of the following is a sign of: tearing the clothes; not shaving or wearing make-up; a plain coffin.
   c) Do you think it is better to talk about something you feel very sad about or to keep it to yourself? Give your reasons.
   d) Why do you think the Kaddish praises God and does not mention the dead person?
4 a) How do you think the Russian Jews in the wedding photograph feel? Explain the reasons for your answer.
   b) Write a paragraph describing a wedding or funeral you have been to. If it was not in a synagogue, point out which things were the same and which were different.

▶ Everything that happens in this world happens at the time God chooses. The time for planting and the time for pulling up.

Ecclesiastes 3:1–2

Seeds are sown; the sun shines; the rain falls; the seeds sprout; the plants grow. This is the seasonal **cycle**. It happens every year. If the cycle is broken, people will not have enough food. Jews celebrate the seasonal cycle with the festivals of Pesach, Shavuot and Sukkot.

Pesach – the Spring Festival

Spring-cleaning in a Jewish home means making the house ready for Passover. This is when Jews remember the Exodus.

There is a special meal and service at home. To make it easier to follow what happens, everyone has a book called the Haggadah. Often the Exodus story is told in pictures, and the book also has hymns and songs.

Children take a special part in the Passover feast. The youngest asks, 'Why is this evening different from all other evenings?'

The oldest person in the family then reads the story of the Exodus. This includes the final plague. God sent his angels to kill the eldest child in each Egyptian house. The Hebrews had to kill a lamb and smear its blood on their doorposts. Then the angels would 'pass over' their houses. So the Jews call the event Pesach, which means Passover.

Karen describes part of the evening in an Orthodox family.

▶ We have a song which tells about all the things which God did for us at the coming out of Egypt. After each one we sing 'Dayanu'. This means 'it would have been enough'.

If he'd just taken us out, if he'd just opened the Red Sea, if he'd just given us food to eat, it would have been enough. At the end of each verse the children all shout out 'Dayanu!'

The evening is a mixture of sadness and joy. The Jews do not forget that they were once slaves. But they celebrate their freedom with a splendid meal, story-telling and singing. It means a late night for the children, but they look forward to it very much. In Karen's community they make sure that nobody is left out.

▶ We always have friends or relatives or people we don't even know to our **Seder** table. This is an occasion when we like to invite strangers, people who don't have anywhere to go, so that everybody has a Seder service to attend.

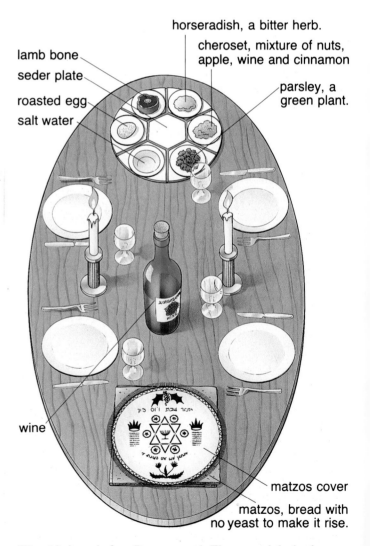

horseradish, a bitter herb.

cheroset, mixture of nuts, apple, wine and cinnamon

lamb bone

seder plate

roasted egg

salt water

parsley, a green plant.

wine

matzos cover

matzos, bread with no yeast to make it rise.

The table is ready for a Passover meal. The egg and the lamb are not eaten.

Sukkot – the Harvest Festival

The Jews who left Egypt with Moses did not have settled homes. They travelled for forty years in the desert. Their homes were **temporary** ones which they build to protect themselves from the weather, wild animals and enemies.

These shelters were called sukkot. They were not very strong. The Jews relied on God to protect them.

Jews today remember that God looked after their ancestors in the desert. Some modern Jews build sukkot in their gardens or help to build one in the synagogue. Karen describes the Sukkot celebrations in her family.

▶We build a sukkah because the children love it and because it's another way for them to live the religion. Those of us who build sukkot, we have great parties, we have what's called a sukkah-crawl. We go from one sukkah to another and we drink wine and eat fruit. It's absolutely delightful.

We eat in there and the children have their breakfast in there. But we don't sleep in there. However, in Israel, they do live in the sukkah.

Building a sukkah.

Jews carry branches of palm, myrtle and willow, and citron fruit, during the festival of Sukkot. They wave them up and down and to north, south, east and west. It shows that God is everywhere.

1 a) Look at the picture of the Passover table.
b) Write each named item on a separate line and miss a line between each.
c) Next to it, copy out from the list below what each item is a reminder of. The first one is done for you.
roasted egg: Jews used to take an offering of food to the Temple.
the Jews left Egypt in a hurry – no time for bread to rise;
the slaves mixed cement for building;
salt tears of Jews in slavery;
bitter memories of hard times in Egypt;
lamb's blood was smeared on Hebrew doors;
Passover celebrates new life for Jews and all growing things;
a drop is spilt to remember the unhappiness caused by each plague.
d) Draw your own picture of the Seder table.
2 Why do some Jews build sukkot in their gardens or synagogues?
3 Describe the part you think God played in the events remembered at Passover, Shavuot (page six) and Sukkot. Write a paragraph for each.

New Year is the time when Jews celebrate the creation of the world. They call it Rosh Hashanah. It comes on the first day of the Jewish month of Tishri, in September or October. The Jewish year 5750 began on 30 September 1989.

► These are days in which we look back and ask ourselves 'Have we really done what we were meant to do?' If we find **shortcomings** we should feel a sense of [guilt] and resolve 'Never again! Next year we'll be better'.

Lord Jakobovits

There is a special New Year meal. The family dip their first piece of bread in honey and say, 'May God give me a sweet and happy New Year'. They have apples dipped in honey, too.

Jews believe that God keeps a Book of Life. It has the names of everyone who is sorry for doing wrong. Many families send Rosh Hashanah cards with the message 'May you be written in the Book of Life'.

God decides on the first day of the year who will be forgiven, but anyone who is left out has ten days to show he is truly sorry. During that time, Jews try to apologise to everybody they have been unkind to.

God makes his final judgement on Yom Kippur, which means Day of **Atonement**. Jews have a good meal the night before, because this is a day on which they do not eat or drink. Giving up something important is a sign that you are really sorry for doing wrong.

Synagogues are packed on Rosh Hashanah and Yom Kippur. They are called the High Holydays because they are the most important festivals in the Jewish year. Lord Jakobovits, who was the British Chief Rabbi, sent this message for Rosh Hashanah.

► I wish my fellow Jews and, through them, my fellow men, 'Shana Tovah', a good New Year. May we contribute to the wonderful world into which we were created.

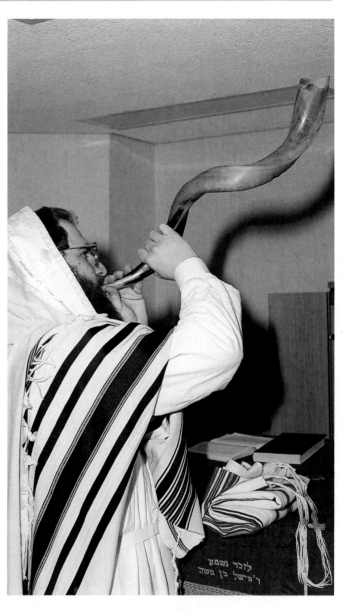

The Shofar or ram's horn is sounded to call Jews to the synagogue during Rosh Hashanah. Why do you think a ram's horn is used?

Simchat Torah

Simchat Torah comes at the end of Sukkot. It means Rejoicing of the Law. Simchat Torah is the most cheerful day in the Jewish year. It is the day when the reading of the Torah comes to an end and starts again. Karen describes Simchat Torah in her Orthodox synagogue.

▶ As soon as we have finished reading the scroll, we immediately roll it back to the beginning and start all over again.

We take out all the Scrolls of the Law from the Ark. They're taken round the synagogue seven times. We do it once in the morning and once in the evening.

The children all have flags and they have apples on their flags. The women throw nuts and raisins and sweets down and the children can eat them. They sing and they dance, because it's a celebration of the cycle of life and of our marriage to the Torah.

There's a big party for all the congregation. The children stay all day. They have a puppet show and a magician.

We've had two very serious festivals recently, Rosh Hashanah and Yom Kippur, and it's a good way of rounding off the whole of the High Holyday season with a lovely party. It's the event of the year

A Simchat Torah procession. Notice the Torah scrolls.

1 a) Draw this grid in your book and fill in the answers, using the clues opposite.

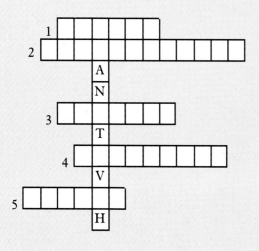

(1) Celebrates the Exodus.
(2) Jewish New Year.
(3) Celebrates the giving of the Law.
(4) Day of Atonement.
(5) Ram's horn.
b) Now, write the words which go down and explain what they mean.

2 a) Explain in your own words why the High Holydays are so important for Jews.
b) What is the difference between atonement and just saying you are sorry?
c) Do you think it is a good idea to try to remember things you have done wrong? Give your reasons.

3 a) Why do you think Karen calls Simchat Torah 'the event of the year'?
b) Write a paragraph about your 'event of the year'.
c) Now draw a picture of it.

▶ Whenever the Jews on earth rejoice in their festivals, they give praise to the Lord. They put on fine clothes, and pile their tables with good food. So the angels ask, 'Why do the Jews pamper themselves so much?' And God answers, 'They have an important Guest today. I am with them.

Writings of the Rabbis

The last Channukah candle of the evening is lit. Can you tell which day of the festival it is?

The Torah tells the Jews to hold the festivals of Passover, Shavuot and Sukkot. But there are other festivals which have become traditions. A tradition is a custom which one **generation** passes on to the next.

Two festivals remind Jews of people who risked their lives for Judaism. At about the time of the Christian festival of Christmas, Jews have a celebration which children love. It is Channukah, the Festival of Lights.

Channukah celebrates an event which happened two thousand years ago. The Syrian Greeks had conquered the Jews. They would not allow them to worship God. They put them to death if they read the Torah.

After years of fighting, a group of Jews managed to defeat the Greeks and drive them out of Jerusalem. They were free to worship again.

One of the first things they needed to do was relight the lamp in the Temple. There was only enough oil for one night and it would take eight days to get some more. They lit it anyway. But after one day, the lamp was still alight. It remained burning for eight days!

At Channukah, Jews have a special candlestick. It has places for eight candles plus a servant candle which is used for lighting the rest. They light one candle on the first evening, two on the second and so on.

It has become traditional to have parties and for children to be given presents. Schoolchildren sometimes put on Channukah plays.

These children are acting out the story of Esther. Which characters can you pick out?

There is another time when Jewish children dress up and act out a story. It is called Purim and falls in February or March.

It's a time when Jews remember Esther. Esther was Queen of Persia. She was also Jewish, but her husband did not know this. The King's chief minister was Haman. He hated the Jews.

These cakes are called Haman's Ears! When do you think they are eaten?

Esther's uncle would not bow down to Haman. Haman was so angry that he plotted to have all the Jews killed, and he **drew lots** to decide on the date. The Hebrew word for lots is Purim.

Anyone who went to see the King without permission was put to death. But Esther dared to go and tell her husband of Haman's wickedness. The King forgave her for breaking the law and Haman was put to death.

The full story is in the Book of Esther in the Tenach. It is read out in the synagogue. Every time Haman's name is mentioned, the children stamp their feet, boo and hiss and shake rattles. They're trying to drown out Haman's name. It is rather like a pantomime, where everyone boos the villain.

After the synagogue service, some children put on fancy dress and visit Jewish houses. They collect money for charity. They may sing:

▶ Today is Purim, tomorrow no more.
Give me a penny.
I'll be gone from your door.

1 a) Draw a series of pictures to tell the story of Esther.
   b) Do you think Esther was brave? Give your reasons.
2 a) Why do you think it is important for Jews to remember the events of Purim and Channukah?
   b) Write about a tradition your family keeps every year. It need not be connected with religion.
3 Light is important in many religious and non-religious rituals.
   a) Why do you think this is so?
   b) Write down at least four occasions you know of when light is used for a special reason.

| nun | gimmel | heh | shin |

The first letters of a Hebrew sentence which means 'A great miracle happened here.'

4 a) You need a piece of stiff card about five cms square. Write one of the Hebrew letters above on each side of the square.
   b) Make a small hole in the middle and push a used matchstick through it. You have a dreidel, a kind of spinning-top. Jewish children play games with them at Channukah.
5 Play this game in fours. You will need a dreidel and a box of counters or similar objects. Each player has six counters, twelve stay in the box. Spin the dreidel in turn.
If Nun comes at the top it means take nothing.
If Gimmel comes up it means take all.
If Heh comes up it means take half.
If Shin comes up it means put one in.
When you have nothing left, you are out.
If there's only one or no objects left in the box, everyone has to put one in. Play on until one player has everything.

14 Young People and Judaism

▶ The world exists only through the breath of schoolchildren.

The Talmud

If people stopped having children the human race would die out. Of course, that is not very likely. But if people stopped learning how to make computers or play tennis those skills would die out, and it would not be easy to start them off again.

If Jewish children did not learn about Judaism from their parents and teachers, then their religion and way of life would come to an end. The reason there are still Jews today, thousands of years after Abraham, is that adults have shown their children how to follow the Jewish faith.

Karen and Rosalind belong to Orthodox communities. Their children are aged between three and twelve. One of Karen's favourite verses in the Torah is, 'You shall teach them (the commandments) to your children'. Rosalind gave this reason for wanting her children to learn about Judaism.

▶ The children must be educated to understand their culture, traditions and religion. Then they can at least choose with knowledge. They can marry Jews or not, be Orthodox or not, [knowing] what they are taking on.

Solving a problem at a Jewish Youth Club.

Children of all ages enjoy life at camp.

Jewish children learn a lot at home, but they can also go to religion school. Some young people go until they are nineteen. They take Jewish Studies and can train as teachers. They help with the younger classes, telling Bible stories and teaching the Hebrew alphabet.

But it's not all hard work! There are Jewish youth clubs, too. They often organise camps so that young people can meet Jews from outside their neighbourhoods. This is what one teenage girl wrote about the camps she has attended.

▶ The camps are incredible fun. At the camps there are themes throughout the week. Themes that have been used at camp are Israel, Kibbutz, Jews around the world, and learning about the **Holocaust**. I have been attending the camps since I was seven and every year I enjoy them more and more.

Her youth group also goes to camps in Israel. One of the aims of the camps is to persuade young Jews to live in Israel. The summer camps give them a chance to find out what it is like.

Young Jews have their own page in the *Jewish Chronicle*, a weekly newspaper. One section is called Junior Chronicle. It has competitions, quizzes and news of Jewish schools and playgroups.

The other part of the page is Young Idea. This is for teenagers. Its items range from news of Jewish pop groups to reports of fund-raising activities.

Members of the Link group enjoy a musical get-together with old friends.

Many young Jews work for the Jewish Welfare Board. It is sometimes called the JWB for short. Members of the JWB raise money for elderly and disabled people in the Jewish community.

The youth groups have names like Vital Sparks, Link and Life. They enjoy meeting the people they help to raise money for. Joanne belongs to Vital Sparks.

▶ We go regularly every month. We have tea with the people in the home, and a singsong. That way we don't lose sight of what we are aiming for.

1 a) Write a sentence to describe how Jewish children learn about Judaism.
b) Why is it important that they do this? Give at least two reasons.
c) What is Rosalind's reason?
d) Do you think it is a good one? Explain your answer.

2 a) Which of these words do you think describe the Jewish camps? Give a reason for each choice.
fun; boring; friendly; interesting; expensive; dangerous; happy.
b) Where else can young Jews meet each other?

c) Where do you meet young people who have the same interests as you?
d) Write a paragraph describing one of your interests.

3 a) Write down the names of some young JWB groups.
b) Why do you think they chose those names?
c) Think of at least three other names for groups of young people who help the elderly or disabled.
d) Do you think it is a good idea for young people to help them? Give reasons.

There have been Jewish communities in Britain for over three hundred years. Now there are more than 300 000 Jewish people here. Most of them live in London or other big cities. This is what three Jewesses feel about being Jewish in a non-Jewish country.

▶ I think many communities, particularly outside large cities, are similar to ours. We all (except two families) drive and use electricity on Saturday. We send our children to English state schools, eat non-kosher meat and bread and drink non-kosher milk.

And yet we remain a community. We have social gatherings and festival services, celebrations and parties.

▶ Practical difficulties are the problems about buying kosher food in **rural** areas. Also most shops are open on Saturdays (our Sabbath) and closed on Sundays (our weekday).

Children must make their own way as individuals who are different in school from as early as the age of five. This can be [upsetting], especially at Christmas time.

▶ As a Jew I have found no problems. Many Jews are well-**integrated** into non-Jewish society while able to retain their Jewishness. Many [of us] talk to groups and individuals about Judaism and invite friends to share in Jewish festivals and services.

Most Jews mix freely with non-Jews at work or school or in their neighbourhood. This does not mean that they feel less strongly about their Judaism, as this Orthodox teenager explains.

▶ I do not think that being Jewish affects my friendships because most of my friends are non-Jewish. But I would not get into a serious relationship with a non-Jewish boy and I shall definitely marry a Jew.

An important part of Jewish life is helping other people. The Jewish Welfare Board has served the Jewish Community for over 125 years. Its **logo** makes its aims clear.

Members of Karen's synagogue volunteer to help both Jews and non-Jews.

▶ We support a local Jewish mentally-handicapped home. Many of our community are 'aunties and uncles' there. They take the children home for tea, or they take them out for the afternoon.

We operate trolleys and the visitors' shop at the local hospital. But that's not just the Jewish community. It's organised by the Red Cross and we have a day for doing it.

Jews who live near this Kosher shop in North London can do their shopping on Sundays.

The Council of Christians and Jews was founded in Britain in 1942. Its main aim is for Christians and Jews to understand each others' religions. It hopes to make sure that, in future, people will not be **prejudiced** against members of different religions. Madeleine's experience suggests that this is happening.

▶ I personally have felt in recent years a desire among sections of the non-Jewish community to learn about and understand the Jewish religion. Many in my community feel strongly about understanding other **minorities** and being understood.

The Archbishop of Canterbury called for Christians and Jews to act together. This was his reason:

▶ The shared belief in One God is a **summons** to us to speak again and again together to the modern world.

Hasidic Jewish boys in Jerusalem. Wherever they live they cover their heads at all times. The hair at the side of their heads is left long.

Leaders from Christian, Buddhist, Hindu and Jewish faiths meet in friendship.

1 a) What problems do Jewish rules create for adult Jews in Britain?
b) How do some Jews help other people to understand Judaism?
c) What problems may there be for Jewish children?
d) How do you think non-Jewish children can help them?
2 a) What are the aims of the Jewish Welfare Board?
b) Name some of the ways in which money is raised.
c) In groups, plan a fund-raising event for a local Day Centre for the elderly.
d) Choose a name for your group and design a logo for it.
e) As a class, decide which is the best fund-raising idea. Remember it will need to raise money and be enjoyable for the people taking part.
3 If you are Jewish, perhaps your teacher will arrange for you to tell the class about some aspect of Judaism in Britain which interests you.

▶ So long as you can feel
the cold –
the wet –
the hunger,
and the lice –
which itch,
and drink your blood
You are alive –
Rejoice
You will survive
Be strong,
it can't be long.

        Michael Etkind, a survivor of the Holocaust.

Jews praying at the Western Wall in Jerusalem. This is the only part of the Temple which the Romans did not destroy.

In 70CE, the Romans attacked the Holy City of Jerusalem, the centre of the Promised Land. They destroyed the Temple. Hundreds of thousands of Jews were killed and many carried off to Rome as slaves.

▶ It's hard to understand what the loss of Jerusalem, and especially the Temple, meant to those Jews of old. It was so much more than just blocks of stone to them.
To begin with, they believed with all their hearts that the '**divine** presence' inhabited the Temple. They believed that when it was destroyed by the Romans, this presence left it – and where was it then to be found?

        Lynne Reid Banks: *Letters to my Israeli Sons.*

The Temple has never been rebuilt. After its destruction, the Jews were scattered in countries all over the Middle East and Europe. This scattering is called the Diaspora. Many people hated the Jews or were afraid of them. This may have been because the Jews were different from them in some ways.

Jews in the Middle Ages sometimes had to wear special clothes to make them look different.

Hatred of Jews is called anti-Semitism. One of the most terrible examples of this took place in Europe before and during the Second World War. Hitler, the leader of Germany, thought that Jews were almost sub-human and wanted to destroy them all.

Anne Frank was a Jewish girl living in Amsterdam. For nearly three years she kept a diary. This extract will give you some idea of what life was like for Jews in Holland after the Germans **occupied** it in 1940.

▶ Jews must wear a yellow star, Jews must hand in their bicycles, Jews are banned from trams and are forbidden to drive. Jews are forbidden to visit theatres, cinemas, and other places of entertainment. Swimming baths, tennis courts and other sports grounds are all prohibited to them. Jews may not visit Christians.

In 1942, the Nazis began rounding up Jews in Germany and occupied countries in Europe. For two years, Anne and her family lived in hiding in Amsterdam. In all that time she did not give up hope.

▶ In spite of everything I still believe that people are really good at heart. If I look up into the heavens, I think that it will all come right. Peace will return again.

These women, in Belsen concentration camp, are using the boots and shoes of people who have been murdered, as fuel.

The Nazis took the Jews to **concentration camps**. The strongest had to work like slaves. Many died from disease or starvation. The majority were gassed or shot, and burned. The Nazis caused the deaths of twelve million people. Nearly half of them were Jews. This mass-murder is called the Holocaust.

The Franks' hiding-place was discovered in August 1944. Anne Frank died in Belsen concentration camp in March 1945. She was fifteen.

At Dachau, in Germany, one of the concentration camps is now a museum. On the wall is written, in French, English, German and Russian, the words:

NEVER AGAIN

Many people, not only Jews, are determined that young people will learn about what happened. They hope that this will prevent anything like it happening again.

Karen is an Orthodox Jewess who goes into schools to talk about Judaism.

▶ Perhaps one day one of those children that I speak to might meet someone who doesn't do things quite the way they do things. Who maybe won't eat the same food as they eat; who maybe has their head covered.

And perhaps they will understand why, and they will **tolerate** it. And it just might make the world a little easier to live in.

1 Which of these words describe Michael Etkind or Anne Frank or both? Give a reason for each choice.
hopeful; greedy; brave; strong; desperate; trusting; unkind; stupid; afraid; patient.

2 a) Using your own words, write a paragraph on what life was like for Jews in a country occupied by the Germans.
b) Draw a picture strip to show four things Jews were not allowed to do.

3 a) Write a sentence describing how you think the Jews felt when their Temple was destroyed.
b) Write a paragraph describing how you think the Jews felt when they had to go and live in another country.
c) Think of at least two problems they may have had.
d) How do you think you could help strangers in Britain? Think of at least two ways.

4 a) Why do you think we should remember the Holocaust?
b) Suggest at least two ways in which we can make sure people remember.

17 . . . Going Back. . .

Jews around the world always hoped that Israel would become the Jewish homeland once more. About a hundred years ago, small numbers began going back. They bought land from the Arabs and started farming. They were called the Pioneers. The Jewish National Fund was set up to help to buy land for the early settlers.

▶ Most of it came, in the form of small coins and crumpled, grubby notes, out of thousands upon thousands of little blue boxes. These were the collection-boxes of the JNF.

Nearly every Jewish home and shop and factory had one. Few Jewish workers were too poor, or Jewish children too selfish, to drop their dollar bills or sixpence or pennies through the slot on Fridays.

Lynne Reid Banks: *Letters to my Israeli Sons*

In Israel, groups of Jews joined one another to run the farms. They decided to share everything. The money they earned was put together and used for everyone's benefit. Each farm was called a kibbutz.

Today there are nearly two hundred and fifty kibbutzim in Israel. Sharing is still the most important part of the life there. Nobody owns their own land or property. But everybody has somewhere to live and nobody goes short of food or clothes.

Everyone eats in the dining-hall, and there is usually one television room for everybody. Children go to school on the kibbutz. All those who are strong enough, work. Most of the work is still farming, but there are other jobs to be done, as Sol explains.

▶ I'm taking my turn in the dining-room. All the men on the kibbutz take a three month turn. I teach chemistry at the kibbutz high school. This year I've stopped teaching, come back to work on the kibbutz.

The whole kibbutz idea is based on this. All work is essential. There is no reason on earth why some people should be serving me for years and years, making my breakfast and cleaning the table after me. Why shouldn't I have a go of it?

Right: Learning to care for animals on a modern kibbutz.

Babies and young children are looked after during the day so that both their parents can work. The people in charge of the children buy and look after their clothes and give them most of their meals. When the family gets together in the evening they can just relax and chat or play games together.

Madeleine spent a year and a half living on a kibbutz. This is how she remembers it.

▶ As [most] of the older members came from English-speaking countries, I soon felt very much at home. There was a tremendous community spirit, with everyone sharing in the joys and griefs of other members. It was like a huge family.

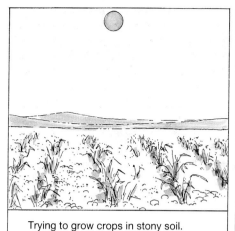

Trying to grow crops in stony soil.

Many pioneers had never been farmers.

Danger from Arabs.

Not enough food.

Fetching water in barrels.

No houses – rain or wind blew down tents in winter.

Life on an early kibbutz.

1 a) Why was the Jewish National Fund set up?
b) Where did the money come from?
c) Do you think it is a good idea for poor people to give away their money? Give reasons.

2 a) Copy the pictures of life on an early kibbutz.
b) Write a paragraph describing that life.
c) Why do you think people were prepared to put up with the difficulties?

3 a) Why will knowing how to care for animals be useful for the children in the picture when they are adults?
b) Name at least three things about life on a kibbutz which are different from your family's life in England.
c) Give at least two advantages and two disadvantages of life on a kibbutz.
d) Why do you think people go to live on a kibbutz?
e) Would you like to? Give reasons.

18 ... *To The Promised Land*...

▶ Next year in Jerusalem.

Seder Service

Thousands of Jews lost their homes during the Second World War. Afterwards, many countries agreed that the Jews should have a land of their own; the land which God promised to them at the time of Abraham. So the State of Israel was set up in 1948. Amiram was nine years old at the time.

▶ It was during the night. We were asleep and everybody was listening to the only radio in the kibbutz. When the news came they woke us up and brought us to the dining-hall. Everybody was dancing. We were in our pyjamas and on our parents' shoulders.

Jerusalem is a holy city for Jews, Christians and Muslims. Look for the dome of the Muslim mosque and the cross on top of the Christian church.

▶ And so it was that on the morning of June 7 1967, going with the paratroopers, I stood for the first time at the (Western) Wall. At Judaism's most sacred shrine. And I, who am not an observant Jew, covered my head and wept. As all the ancestors back through all the generations of Jews that link me to Abraham would have done.

STAR OF DAVID

STRIPES OF TALLIT

The Israeli flag. David was the King who made Jerusalem the centre of Israel three thousand years ago.

Not everyone accepted the State of Israel. Arabs had lived in **Palestine** for two thousand years. They did not want to hand part of their land over to the Jews. Since 1948 there has been a number of wars between Israel and her Arab neighbours.

In the Six-Day War of June 1967, the Israelis captured the part of Jerusalem which had been in Arab hands since 1948. The importance of this success was summed up by Michael Elkins.

The problem of the land of Israel is still not solved. Some Arabs and Jews will not accept any attempts at a peaceful settlement. There are attacks on Israel by Arabs of the Palestine **Liberation** Organisation. Israeli troops attack the Arabs.

Jews have different feelings about how much land should belong to Israel. Some believe that it must be everything which God promised, even though this means less land for the Arabs. Others feel that it may be worth settling for less for the sake of peace.

▶ Israel was given by God to the Jewish people. I believe in the biblical **boundaries** of the State of Israel.

Malvyn Benjamin, Orthodox

▶ I agree that Israel is a God-given land. But my religious beliefs do not include an idea of boundaries as being more important than peace.

Charles Emmanuel, Reform

The Jews will not give up the land God promised them. They will continue to try to reach agreement with all their Arab neighbours. Then their Promised Land will be at peace.

▶ The State of Israel is so very important because it is the true home of the Jews. Being Jewish is not just a religion. It is also a nationality.

I think that after all our forefathers have been through to keep our homeland, everyone should make **aliyah** there. I feel strongly about returning to Israel, so strongly that I am returning once I am eighteen.

Orthodox girl

Schoolchildren in Israel plant young trees on New Year's Day For Trees. Trees are important in Israel because they give protection from the weather, stop the soil from being blown away, and provide timber and food.

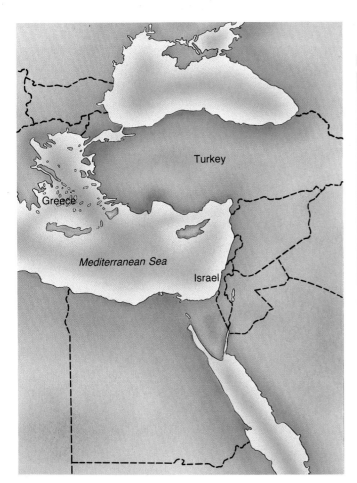

The Middle East today.

1 a) Copy the flag of Israel.
b) Why do you think it has the Star of David and the lines on it?
2 a) Copy the map of the Middle East into your book.
b) Using an atlas, name the Arab countries which border Israel. How many are there?
c) Why did the Arabs object to the setting-up of the State of Israel?
d) Do you think it was right for the Jews to be given land where Arabs had lived for many years? Try to give reasons for 'and against.
3 a) Why was the recapture of the whole of Jerusalem important to the Israelis?
b) Why do you think Jews go to pray at the Western Wall? Page 36 may help.
4 Read all the quotations.
a) Write down the names of each person.
b) Write a sentence for each, describing what you think are their feelings about Israel.

Torah scrolls in a synagogue in Egypt.

There are about fourteen million Jews today. They live in many different countries. Nearly a quarter live in Israel, but the USA has more Jews than anywhere else. New York alone has a Jewish population of just under two million.

Jews have been affected by the countries they live in and the people they have met. Their beliefs have not changed, but some of their traditions may be different.

In most countries, Jews are free to live as they wish. They can meet in synagogues, hold festivals and study the Torah without being afraid.

However, this is not true everywhere. In the Soviet Union, for example, life is difficult for Jewish people. Many synagogues have been closed. But many Jews keep their beliefs and live the Jewish way of life as far as they can.

One problem is that the government will only allow a very small number of Jewish books to be published. So, when there was an Israeli stand at the 1987 Moscow Book Fair, Jews from all over the Soviet Union went there.

They went to see the books about Israel and Judaism on display. It was also a chance to talk to other Russian Jews and to the Jews who had come from Israel to show the books. Read what one Israeli said.

▶ I will never forget a fourteen-year-old boy who had travelled a thousand miles by train to get to the fair. He had queued for five hours and then had less than an hour to look at the books and talk to the Israelis before setting off on his return journey – clutching a Magen (Star of) David we gave him.

Many Russian Jews would like to live in Israel or America. They have to ask for permission to leave Russia. At first the government may refuse, so these Jews are known as refuseniks. One man waited twenty years before he was allowed to leave.

Jews and non-Jews in many countries try to persuade the Soviet Union to allow more Russian Jews to leave. They write letters to the Soviet Government. They hold demonstrations so that people will know what is happening.

This man is wearing traditional Indian costume in the synagogue in Cochin.

Elana Friedman stands in Jerusalem surrounded by pictures of her sister, Ida Nudel.

Ida has been a refusenik for sixteen years. Elana wants her to be able to join her in Israel.

There is a happy ending to her story. Her sister was finally given permission to go to Israel. Ida had this message for her supporters.

▶ I thank people of goodwill the world over, from Presidents and Prime Ministers to people from all walks of life. I want to thank all of you who **campaigned** for me.

Never feel that your struggle is in vain. All those years, I felt the sympathy from thousands of people, Jews and non-Jews alike. You must continue the struggle.

Some Jews in Russia have been put in prison for criticising things which they do not agree with. Nathan Sharansky was imprisoned for nine years. He was released in 1986 and allowed to go to Israel. During his time in prison, he had a book of Psalms which his wife had given him.

It was taken away from him because the prison officers thought religion was a bad influence. Sharansky would not give in. The book was very important to him.

▶ Through this I felt my connection with my wife, with my people, my history, with God. It helped me to feel myself together with my wife and with my people during all those years. I started strikes. I refused to work. In that year I spent 186 days in the punishment cell. But finally they returned the Psalm book to me.

1 a) How can you tell that the Indian in the picture on the opposite page is in a synagogue?
b) Think of at least two ways in which people's lives might change when they go to live in another country.
c) How might life be difficult for them if they did not change?
d) Write down at least two ways in which you and your family could help a family from another country who moved to live next door.
e) Write down any reasons you can think of why strangers may not seem to want your help.
2 a) For each of the following, write a sentence to say what they did to get something they really wanted:
the Jewish teenager; Elana Friedman; Nathan Sharansky.
b) Who do you think had the most difficult task? Give reasons.
3 a) Imagine you are a fourteen-year-old Jew in Russia. You have just arrived home from a trip to the Moscow Book Fair. Write a letter to an English pen-friend explaining why you thought it was worth travelling a thousand miles to spend less than an hour there.
b) Now write a letter in rely. Tell your Russian pen-friend about something *you* really wanted to do. Describe what you had to do to achieve your ambition.

20 *Judaism's Gifts to the World*

▶ The Law of Moses has changed them that come into contact with it, even though they seem to have cast the Law aside.

Yehuda Halevi, twelfth century Jewish poet

The way you talk and dress and eat and think can all be affected by other people. For example, you speak English because most people in this country do.

Judaism has influenced many people's lives. If you are a Muslim or a Christian you may have spotted that Judaism has some things in common with your religion. The most important is that they share the belief in one God. But there are other links.

The Tenach is the Old Testament of the Christian Bible. You may have heard the stories of Noak's Ark, Jonah and the Whale, and Daniel in the Lions' Den. These are all tales from Jewish Holy Books. Some of the characters in the Muslim holy books and in the Tenach are the same people.

The Ten Commandments are as important to Christians as to Jews. There is a reading from the Old Testament in church services, and Christians sing Psalms, written by the Jewish King David.

There is a good reason why so many things are the same. All three religions can trace their beginnings back to Abraham.

Jesus Christ, the founder of Christianity, was a Jew. He was descended from Abraham and his son, Isaac. Muhammad, the founder of Islam, was an Arab. He was descended from Abraham and his other son, Ishmael.

Flora Solomon lives in a flat in London. She is Jewish. Many of her neighbours are Arabs.

▶ I met one in the lift the other day and I said, 'I am a Jew and you are an Arab so we should be safe from any bombs'. And he said 'Madame, we are cousins,' and he kissed my hand!

Rabbi Gershon Cohen sums up two important effects of Judaism.

▶ Everybody knows that a week is seven days. The Lord rested from His creation on the seventh day. No other people had that [idea] of having a seven day week. That's one of the [gifts of Judaism] to the world at large.

[Another practice that grew up as a result of Judaism is the law of] charity to the poor. You may not neglect any suffering. Let me take one example that made a deep impression upon me as a child. If you see your neighbour's horse or donkey lying collapsed in the street, you may not ignore it. You must help that beast and your neighbour.

Rabbi Julia Neuberger sums up what she thinks is Judaism's main message to its followers and to the world.

▶ I think there is a duty upon you to do God's will. To me, a lot of it is being concerned for the wider community, being concerned for the **oppressed**, the prisoners, looking to the poor. It seems to me that that's the great message of Judaism.

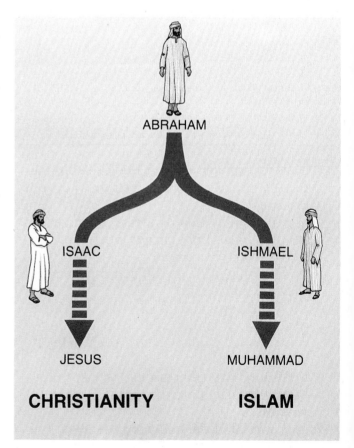

Abraham's family tree.

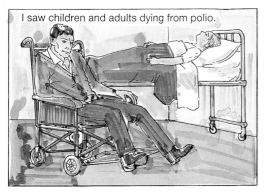

I saw children and adults dying from polio.

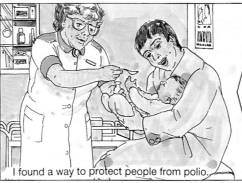

I found a way to protect people from polio.

I AM JONAS SALK.

I met people who had terrible nightmares.

They became ill.

I helped them to understand their dreams and get better.

I AM SIGMUND FREUD.

I began selling buttons and thread from a tray.

Don't ask the price – it's a penny

I teamed up with Tom Spencer to become Marks and Spencer.

I AM MICHAEL MARKS.

A 'Who Am I?' of famous Jews.

---

1 a) Copy Abraham's family tree.
b) Explain how Judaism, Islam and Christianity are linked.
c) Give examples of at least two things which are the same in Judaism and one other religion.

2 Choose two Jews who have helped to make life better in some way.
a) Write down what each of them did.
b) Write down two words which you think describe each person.

c) Describe what might happen now if those people had not lived.

3 a) Choose two more people who have done something special to help others. They do not have to be Jewish.
b) For each one, write a paragraph about what they did.
c) For each one, draw a series of pictures to show how they helped others.

4 Which do you think is the most important gift Judaism has given to the world? Give reasons.

Connections

1 This square contains seventeen words connected with Judaism. Each one has appeared in this book. They could read up, down or sideways. Each time you find one, write it down and write a sentence about it.

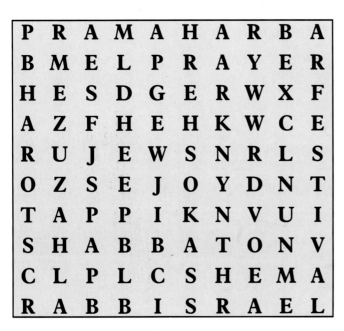

P	R	A	M	A	H	A	R	B	A
B	M	E	L	P	R	A	Y	E	R
H	E	S	D	G	E	R	W	X	F
A	Z	F	H	E	H	K	W	C	E
R	U	J	E	W	S	N	R	L	S
O	Z	S	E	J	O	Y	D	N	T
T	A	P	P	I	K	N	V	U	I
S	H	A	B	B	A	T	O	N	V
C	L	P	L	C	S	H	E	M	A
R	A	B	B	I	S	R	A	E	L

2 a) Write a newspaper headline for an event remembered at each of these festivals. The first one is done for you opposite.

     Purim
     Pesach
     Rosh Hashanah
     Channukah
     Sukkot

b) Choose one Jewish festival. It need not be one from part a).
EITHER: You are a Jewish teenager. Write to a non-Jewish pen-pal. Describe how you celebrated the festival this year.
OR: Write a newspaper article describing the event as it happened thousands of years ago.

3 Here are drawings of objects you should recognise. But the artist has not completed the pictures!
a) Draw each complete object and write its name underneath.
b) Explain what each object means to a Jew.

PERSIAN TIMES

BRAVE QUEEN SAVES THOUSANDS!

From our own reporter
It was announced today
that Queen Es

4 a) Describe the part of Jewish life you think you would i) find easiest and ii) find most difficult to follow. Give reasons.
b) Compare your answers in a class discussion.

Glossary

aliyah – going to live in Israel
Atonement – coming back to God after doing wrong

bimah – raised platform in a synagogue
boundaries – dividing lines between countries

campaigned – did things for a particular reason
circumcised – had loose skin of penis cut off
commandment – order from God
community – group of people
concentration camp – place in which people are forced to stay
conduct – behaviour
congregation – group of people who worship together
creation – everything that was made
cremation – burning
culture – development
cycle – complete set of events

deceased – dead
descendants – members of family who are born after
divine – like God
drew lots – decided by picking from a bag of small objects

famine – lack of food
foundation – what everything else depends on

generation – people born about the same time

headstone – gravestone
holocaust – total destruction

integrated – mixed with

Jewess – female Jew

liberation – freedom
logo – sign

minorities – small groups of people

negate – say it doesn't exist

obligation – what you have a duty to do
observant – obeying the Law
occupied – taken over by force
oppressed – kept down by force

Palestine – ancient home of the Jews
parchment – animal skin prepared for writing on
prejudiced – having an opinion without a good reason

quill – kind of pen

responsibility – what you must do
ritual – to do with religious occasions
rural – country

sacrifice – killing an animal as an offering to God
scribe – writer
Seder – Passover service at home
sermon – speech by minister
Shabbat – Sabbath
shortcomings – failures
Siddur – Jewish prayer-book
signifies – stands for
spiritual – to do with religious things
stable – firm
summons – call
synagogue – Jewish place of meeting

temporary – for a short time
tolerate – allow without interfering
typhoon – violent storm

universe – everything which exists

volunteers – people who do things without pay

welfare – well-being
worship – show respect for God

Index